TURNED CORNERS & JUNIPER BERRIES

by
Martha Bartholomew
18N600 West Hill Rd.
Dundee IL 60118

Sakura Press
4170 N. Marine Drive 20A
Chicago, IL 60613-2341

ISBN 0-9660583-4-8

Excerpts from
The New English Bible,
Copyright © 1972
Oxford University Press
Used by permission

Printed in the United States of America

New Life Printing
1508 S. Main
Algonquin, IL 60102

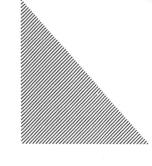

TURNED CORNERS

& JUNIPER BERRIES

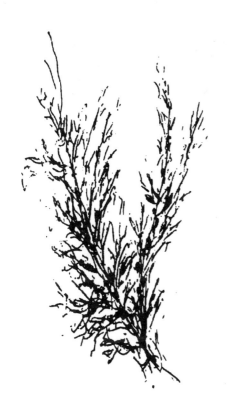

A Poet's Pages for a Reader's Pen

By Martha Bartholomew

Other Books
by Martha Bartholomew

TELLER OF STORY—
      KEEPERS OF DREAM

_____

SEVEN HAIKU
&
SEVENTEEN MORE POEMS

DEDICATION

To

The Poet in Every Person
And most especially to
Lorraine Mark, CSJ
For her faithfulness to
poetry of place
and timelessness of space
Christ in the Wilderness

CONTENTS

~~~~~~~

Illustrations

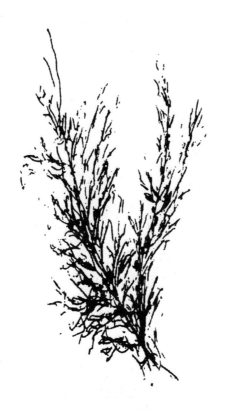

One has to go by the way one does not know.
What is around the corner is only known by taking
the next step ahead.

Fore Words

May this collection of poetry and pages awaiting your pen, pencil or paint be an invitation for you to pause at the turned corners of your own life journey, to harvest its essential flavor and let the Spirit Wind blow away the chaff.

In part, the title TURNED CORNERS came from the turned down corners of my own journal pages. Recovery from a broken leg afforded me the time I had not given my busy self - permission to explore these chronicles. These turned corners were sentinels, marking places I wanted to re-visit, work in process – myself always – but often a poem or fragment of prose. Just one year's worth of journal pages yields a hefty bulge to the upper right-hand corner of my notebooks.

> Stop at the crossroads; look for the ancient paths;
> Ask 'Where is the way that leads to what is good?'
> Then take that way, and you will find rest for yourselves.
> Jeremiah 6:16

TURNED CORNERS also offers a double entendre. While looking for ancient paths, as invited by the prophet, inevitably I arrive at a crossroads, a place where choice <u>must</u> be made. Taking one turn or another may lead to detours on the adventure, even bridges out, but ultimately it is to discover the ancient way of God's love. I learn to call the way itself "Home". I am held by it, sometimes upon return, having strayed.

Certain patterns emerge giving maps or charts. They often give guidance toward the treasure of my heart's desire. Looking back, I can always note that in the Psalter of life lived, loved, lamented or celebrated, a perennial prayer is being answered.

Examine me, O God, and know my thoughts
Test me and understand my misgivings.
Watch, lest I follow any path that grieves you.
Guide me in the ancient ways.
Psalm 139

What about Juniper Berries? The juniper can be any one of sixty to seventy species of aromatic trees or shrubs scattered throughout the northern hemisphere. These evergreen cedars generously punctuate the eighty acres of woods and prairie landscape at *Christ in the Wilderness—a Place for Solitude and Reflection* in northern Illinois.

Scattered throughout life there are often certain trees, plants, animals, persons or incidents that catch our attention. They can be icons, God's ways of speaking uniquely to us. These opportunities to hear or see may be lost because we are not prepared to receive them. When we pay attention, the message is often right before us. It is then we experience something of what Elizabeth Barrett Browning wrote:

Earth is crammed with heaven;
every common bush is alive with the fire of God.
Only those who see take off their shoes.
The rest sit around picking blackberries.

Black berries or juniper berries! Whatever is right before our eyes has the potential of being an opening into the one Mystery that ultimately matters - *into the poetry of God being written in our own story.* Wherever today's theorists and scientists explore they find the poet has been there already.

A lush berried Juniper encountered on a walk during a late summer retreat provides rich parable and metaphor for plucking during subsequent seasons (sometimes, quite humorously). Spring's scarcely perceptible blossoms have developed into summer's lush blue fruit, legacy of generous rains. Subsequently, fall's rich harvest feeds migrating birds.

Although, in winter the pathway into the Upper Meadow may be impassable, siblings of the "Juniper of note" remain green sentinels above a white blanket near the hermitages. They prove

14

constant reminders of God's ever greening faithfulness amidst the ice and snow of life.

More easily accessible is the tiny cedar lined chapel in a wooded glen. It is made fragrant by the warmth of winter sun upon its roof. I am reminded that cedar juniper is oft times joined in a bundle with sweetgrass, sage or pinon as an incense for ritual blessing among sacred circles. Recently a Navajo woman placed a juniper berry bracelet on my arm. Spirit beads, they are sometimes called. I feel blessed.

Whether an odor to savor, a spice to flavor a gin or a stew, juniper has a history of seasoning life among many cultures. It is known for medicinal qualities as well - a poultice or a tea.

A winter's quiet thought evokes spirits, poems, stories from turned corners. From the gleanings across my seasons, this journal comes with the hope you will make it your own in whatever way it may lead.

Some poems have titles. Many are known only by their first lines. A few are prefaced by background from which they have come. You may wish to pray and play with them as you might a dream, in the manner suggested by the book Dreams and Spiritual Growth.

Title   Give the dream—or the poem, a title.

Theme   Note what theme is present for you

at this reading.

Affect   What feelings awakened in you while you read?

These may change upon subsequent readings.

Question Let the poem ask you a question

rather than asking what it means.

Your journal response will be your own "poetry" for the present. Picture what God is saying to you. Be the scribe of the message you need to hear.

I begin with the fruit of an invitation issued several years ago by writer, mentor, Madeleine L'Engle. She challenged: "Write a story about a formative experience from your childhood, one that touches the numinous."

I touch back to my first "God-memory" and although I may have lacked vocabulary at age four, there is insight undiminished by time. That it happened at a circus does not seem so amazing to me now that I have learned to play again. I can feel fresh, almost childlike, the *Sawdust in My Mary Janes*.

May these poems prime some memories for you and invite you further into the wisdom inherent in your own unique life journey as pilgrim poet. Know God is always present, be it in junipers or whatever, just around some corner waiting to be turned.

Martha Bartholomew

Sabbath Place Hermitage,
Christ in the Wilderness,
Winter/Spring 2001

Browning, Elizabeth Barrett. "Aurora Leigh", Book 7, line 820.
The Complete Works of . . ., Cutchogue, NY: Buccaneer Books, 1993

Louis Savary, Patricia Berne, Strephon K. Williams;
Dreams and Spiritual Growth.Mahwah, NJ 07430, 1984,
Paulist Press, 1984, pg.24

SAWDUST IN MY MARY JANES

Sawdust in my Mary Janes!
My patent party slippers!
Why was I permitted to wear them today?

Mother and her college roommate
    Each firmly held my hands,
    Chattering school chums,
    Replay in reunion,
    Above my curly head.

They were on a holiday,
    Taking me to my first circus.

Sawdust, sounds, sights
    Spun right before my ears and eyes,
    Lifted from the pages of my picture book
        At home.
        It would never be the same!
        Animals larger than life!
        Although, I had been taken to the zoo.

People! A jostling crowd was being swept
    Toward a bright Big-top tent
    By a man wearing a straw hat,
    Pointing with a cane,
        Shouting promises
        Over and over again.

This was not at all like going to church.
    I was being coaxed to laugh, skip, sing!
    I remained as quiet as when in a pew –
        And preferred one to the climb we made

17

Up seemingly rickety open bleachers
                    to our places.
There were narrow red boards on which to sit.
There were narrow red boards on which to stand.
            And wide wide spaces for the falling through
                Of a little girl of four.

"Aren't you having a good time?"
Look! See!
            The elephants!
            The trapeze!
            Dogs jumping through hoops
            The clowns!
                    Aren't they funny?"
I may have nodded without speaking,
                Scarcely picking at my cracker-jack.
                    Never mind about the prize!
            Forgetting sawdust in my shoes
            It was the Clowns!
            They held my gaze,
            But it was not their floppy hats,
            Nor falling down,
            Nor tumbling up and all around
                In baggy clothes,
                Shoes sized 19X ~~~~
                Plenty of room for sawdust
                    Without pinching their toes!
While all around me others laughed
            At rings One, Two or Three,
                I remained the somber child.
My mother and her friend soon resigned –
            "Aren't you having a good Time?,"
                yielding to their own delight.

18

For the first time I could remember
  I was having a very different kind of time.
  Very good, indeed!
Filled with wonder by something not explained,
  Without words to name, scarcely yet proclaim,
    I knew! That long time ago
      I had Seen!
Seen behind the mask of whiteface
  And the antics of a clown
To some shared secret part of each person
  I was ever to meet.
  And~~~
  That something special
  Was to be known best as a part of me!

  I had fallen through~~~
    Fallen through to knowing
    What it was to BE.

                    Martha Bartholomew '87

Spaces for falling

through   ~~~

What is it to BE? ~~~

To be ...
    not dutiful daughter
        ... big sister
            ... good scholar
                ... wife to Jack
                    ... caring mother — of five
                        ... teacher ... principal
                            ... dependable friend

    but

            ME ?

~ ~ ~

20

As the prophet Elijah slept beneath a juniper tree, a fugitive in the wilderness, perhaps he dreamed a poem – a simple rondel? Unlikely? Immaterial. God only knows the poetry of the heart. What form Elijah's cry may have taken is not as important as knowing he was angel met. (I Kings 19) We are told angels of the God camped around them – the tree and the man. He was fed for the long journey that was to be uniquely his. No less are we. No less are we.

Juniper Berries

Juniper Berries

In abundant profusion

Imply an infusion

Invite: Please tarry

Ask solitary

Intimate attention

Juniper berries

In abundant profusion

It's time to fairly

Take pen, dispel illusion

Write, paint, draw to conclusion

Or journal one's query

Other than

Juniper berries.

Fed for the journey

Why do I fear this last part of the
journey? Have I not been "fed for
the journey" all the way along?

The climb to the upper meadow at Christ
in the Wilderness has come to represent
for me this last leg of my journey. The climb
is daunting and takes all my strength.
My prayer each time is for strength
for the journey.

As my body begins to fail me (someday
my mind?) . . . as I see choices narrowing,
my ability to do what I want diminishing
the path I am on becomes clearer and
I know I will need strength for this
journey. God, give me that strength.

~ ~ ~

Traveling Carnival

Once a young friend, a gifted calligrapher received a unique challenge.

As a surprise for her husband, a woman planned to have a plaque installed aboard his boat before he sailed again. The allotted space was measured, quite specific, to the exact quarter inch . The motto was to read:

"Life is an adventure, but then we are not made
for safe havens."

To accommodate the parameters defined and maximize the size of letters, the artist hyphenated the word *"adventure"* to read:

> *Life is an ad-*
> *venture, but*
> *then we are*
> *not made for*
> *safe havens.*

The customer was not pleased, insisting the work be done again. However the rejected original hangs in, above the artist's work space as a reminder that life itself may be gift, an assigned "venture", but what is brought to it in the way of expectation, playfulness and imagination can be value added to make living truly an *ad-venture* whatever the circumstance. In the haven of God's love, we are held.

Perhaps, where but on a carnival midway can we begin to find that invitation to freedom and spontaneity?

Sabbath Place

This place apart
My treetop house
Welcomes me back.

Calming, quieting, enfolding
Filling me with
God's own Peace

With
insight
wisdom
courage
Then sends me forth
Ready for whatever
the future brings.

~ ~ ~

24

Night Flight

What river snakes far below,

luminescent with day's last glow,

yielding to darkening stealth?

Night swallows river, valleys, hills,

towns – their poverty and wealth.

Hymn wind, drone, hum chants vigil.

Wedge wings, tipped red and white,

pulse, slice, probe, promise.

We are held, fated, destined.

Somewhere in between

A discovery!

Below becomes as above.

Countryside constellations,

scattered star blossoms

imitate Orion and his sisters

lost or found in a universe

until we are deposited on the midway

of

The Carnival.

Daring acrobats *in night*

Catch mosquitoes in mid-flight.

Silent stealths in sheaths of air

Sonar conversations spare

Return at dawn to their hangers

Upside down, without much clamor

Fold their wings, snuggle close

Digest while sleeping, dream? Suppose

They're friend to homo sapiens?

At twilight they'll fly again.

Swoop and startle walkers by

Who tell scary tales how and why

Who misread bats best intentions

Cringe with fear spell inventions

About superstitious lore.

Gory untruths told before.

Tree Ring Circus

Squirrels, trapeze artists
of today
Yield to acrobats tonight
Silent, sonar, swift with
stealth
Endanger a mosquito's
health
Bats' bad press gives
needless fright
Blood, once ours, was
skeeter's bite.

Scrub brush

Bedstraw

Cat's tongue

Writing poetry is a cat's tongue

     Licking her litter to life

One black and white

Another gray

A candidate for the Orange Cat Connection

A calico – can't make up her color~mind

Finally - a black, whisker to tail tip

Lucky day!

     ~~~~~~~~~~~~~~~~~~~

Bonasa umbellas *Banana umbrellas?*

     No wonder the grouse is "ruffed"

       miffed

     hiding in the brush.

27

Dr. to Dr. Zeus to M. B.

I am the model of a poet lariat

Lassoing mustangs as wild as they get

Flung, I'm a rope with accurate aim

Missing a few, but its all in the game

It's a round-up of words running wild

      running free

Harness and halter direct energy

In paper corrals they are saddled and ridden

By the One who has thrown rope

      has drawn and has bidden

Their spirit to come, to play rodeo

Entertainment for all who come to the show

I am wound, I am looped, I am sailed overhead

Reeled in and repeated 'til word-horses are bred

To pull wagons and plows through unbroken sod

Joining strong with the weaker

      while reviewers applaud?

Watching the sunset
Her favorite time of day
Remembering Mother

The sun sinks lower
I watch from the high meadow
This day is ending

Stop at the crossroads: look for the ancient paths; ask
'Where is the way that leads to what is good?'
Then take that way and you will find rest for yourselves.

Jeremiah 6:16

~ ~ ~

Journey Train

They who called the wind Moriah
Might name the whistle Jeremiah.
At every crossing, a prophet's wail
Can be heard, must not fail
For travelers perpendicular
To all aboard, in particular.

Seekers of the Ancient Tales.
This path is plotted by steel rails
That lead to where? Ultimate good.
Crossing farm and neighborhood.

Two Friends One Morning

Two Old ladies trudged up the hill

Not early, but the morning chill

From the vestiges of night

Bedewed the grass, gave delight

As Holy Ghostly vapors rose

Inviting first, the short one's nose

Not early, but in morning's chill

Two old ladies climbed up the hill,

One, blue-eyed, the other green

The latter tall, the other Queen

Whose realm is quite inhabited

By creatures – many rabbited.

For two old ladies on the hill
Early isn't quite the thrill
That once it was in yesterdays,
But they have learned much wiser ways.
They listen, look and sniff the air,
Not chasing off to everywhere.

One old lady went down the hill
Much later in the morning. Still
The second stayed, wrote this poem,
She'd later give her friend a bone.

The task of poetry is not to
tell you what happened,

But what happens, not what did
take place,

But the kind of thing that always
does take place.

Northrup Frye

<u>The Educated Imagination</u>

34

FOR LOVE OF POETRY

<u>Centuries</u> of simmering lava-words
    Bubble ~~ ~~ ~~
    Boil to a roar !
    Rise !
    EXPLODE a granite mountaintop!
Ashed air defeats feeble sunlight.
    Volcanic flow
              Hot lava-words

    Tongues
        Lash
              P
          U
            OUT--------→
                      D
                     O
                     W
                     N

            Familiar hillsides
  Sear
   Scour
   Scar
    Score
     Settle
       Cool~~~~~~~~~
          In receptive
          Valleys~~~~~~~~
            Forever change
         Fascicular landscapes.

At 3 o'clock in the afternoon
I'm drunk on poetry and lemonade.
I prepared the way only a little -
    Opened the door a crack,
    Just enough to sweep out distractions
    Was swept off my feet
By a mighty wind of words
    Flooded by torrents
      Inundated

        D
         R
          O
           W
            N
             I
              N
               G

Delightfully
Following green crested lapwings
    And jello fish
To become a hermit crab
    Setting up housekeeping
      In a borrowed notebook shell.

HAIKU

Lazy afternoon

Writing poems and
swatting flies

Life comes and goes

~ ~ ~

To A Muse

RAVEN

Scavenger

Rag and bone picker

Sharp eyed

Hoarder in a treasure nest

Jaunty bird

Your voice is heard

Your raucous cries

     and winged disguise

Blacklight! Surprise!

Funny bird

Mentor Muse

Token Totem

What's the news?

When you appear

A poem lies near for the plucking.

I, a scavenger for words,

Am swift to sift - sort - store

Proclaim: THE WORD.

Am to pluck tarnished treasures

     from the dead—the dying,

Resuscitate Spirit Breath into them

Return trove— burnished— sparkling

     once again

Then fly away with

RAVEN

Friend.

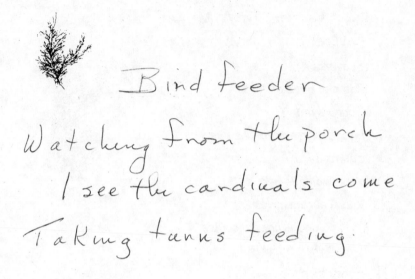

Bird feeder
Watching from the porch
   I see the cardinals come
Taking turns feeding.

      Sabbath Place
I am not alone
   The birds keep me company
In this treetop house.

A DIALOGUE WITH MY MUSE

WRITE! WRITE! WRITE!

Write? Rite?

RIGHT!

A right?

RIGHT! A WRITE RITE!

My Write Rite, right?

RIGHT!

Out of sight!

NO! INSIGHT!

WRITE A WRITE RITE!

The paper is too white.

Fright!

TRY BLUE.

Spill, spell, tell?

RIGHT! RIGHT! RIGHT!

Rite...right...write ...wrote...written.

WRITING, RIGHTING, RIGHTING!

Yeah!!!!!!!!!!

I reach the upper meadow
Breathing hard, I pause to catch
my breath
Glowing red the sumac stands
sentinel waiting for me
My breathing slows and now
my feet take to the path

~ ~ ~

Run for the Hills

The Dam's Busted !

There's gold in them there hills,
Liquid gold, dripped in secret -
The Keeper of the still,

    Mixer of the mash

    Distilling proof,

    Guards – holding shotgun

        Against "revenuers"

    While hoping, in secret

        To be found out

        And better than Jack D.

Gotta jug for poetry?

~ ~ ~

Ode to My purple Pen

Among the sad and solitary
laments is the demise of a pen.
It must now be _re_placed, contrary
to its having been _mis_placed, found again.
Like St. Francis' prayer – made "channel",
Word flow poured: Love, faith, light, and joy
Contrasted: fear, doubt, dark, sadness to spell
Hope, mystery, secrets. Sought by employ
of heart-speak, it welded thought to paper,
was conduit for lists, notices, contracts.
Hand-held, made its point, slave to labor,
evoked curse, blessing, sans ink distracts
a writer from original intent,
is honored by sonnet: a pen well spent.

Some poems

are slippery things
Have misshapen heads
       Like newborns
       After long labor
       Sliding into life
               Wailing, flailing
       Viable with first cry.

Poems are miracles

Outward manifestations
Of an inward grace.
Poems are portraits of soul
On the canvas of life
Brushed from a colorful palette.

Poems are music of the spheres
Composed at the Edge
Cacophony becoming lullaby.

Poems are scales holding balance
Between the expected
And unforeseen.

Silence and solitude make love
Beget poetry through pen, of person
Again and then again.

       Poems are a dance
       Between two or more
       worlds.

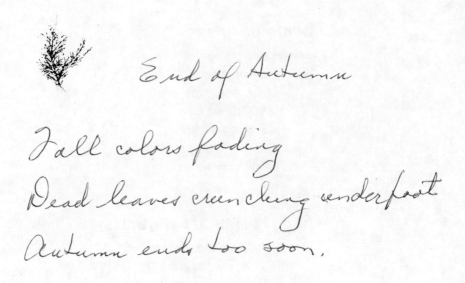

End of Autumn

Fall colors fading
Dead leaves crunching underfoot
Autumn ends too soon.

Solitude

Surrounded by silence
Embracing the quiet
Plus time apart is mine.
Alone, I rediscover me!

~ ~ ~

When I visit my old poetry,

It's like calling on an ancient fond aunt, rocking
In a room too long closed, in need of fresh air,
Of having heavy curtains drawn open
        to sunshine.
I feel a search, the find
Loss – its pain
Once again, recall -
No, more than that -
Remember – re-member in my bones,
        The flesh feel
          A well of tears, not quite dry
          Hear some same questions
              How or Why?
          Taste again, dare, delight
          Sample fear that urges flight.
But no! The Yes is stronger yet.
The essence of what it means
May be less opaque,
Still a magnet to greater mystery
Than back then when
        the pen appeared in the middle of the road,
Back then when
        I wrote more than I knew I knew
And the Yes was simple
        to being a scribe.

The Birdfeeder

Come one! Come all! And come they do.
   Chickadees, dark-eyed juncos, sparrows.
And then the cardinals (he and she)
   And last a tufted titmouse
No pushing, no shoving here ...
   Each takes a turn
Is there a lesson to be learned?

~ ~ ~

Today my name is Rumi.

Shams, in disguise, is vaulting over walls
        Right and left,
        Throwing my books –
        my beloved parchments,
                Into pools - into fountains.
Empty-handed, stripped,
I stand before the hungry in the courtyard,
Discover I am not,
Discover books are naught,
Discover -
        There are pockets in my heartcloth
        Filled with WORD.
Shams' admonition:
        Reach inside!
        Draw out fragments
                Manna,
                Quail
                A small number of loaves
                A fish or two.
Another Voice echoes:
        "Give them something to eat, yourself."
Might this be alchemy -
        To Come – Listen -
                Touch – See - Tell
                Be the Story?

51

LOOKING AROUND

~~~

Trees let loose their leaves
Slowly at first then faster
Soon they will be bare.

~ ~ ~

Haiku II... and YOU too?

Books are paper clips
Gathering together my thoughts
Captured from the wind.

I am so inclined
To watch the woods be defined
By unseen snow brush.

The Universe of God's love
Reflects in a single teardrop
When our world turns Upside down.

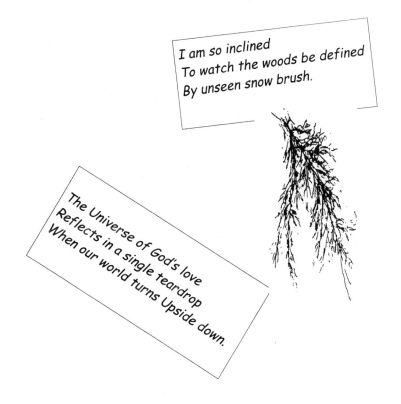

Monday Afternoon in the Park:

Old nun with head tied shut

Against a chill autumn wind

Made her way,

Led me, unbeknown,

From a mourning morning.

Young man, ill, growing old

     before my eyes

Wept compassion for his people.

"It hurts so to leave."

I felt like a mother about to bury a son.

Monday afternoon in the park:

Old nun with cane

Pulls history in her wake

Preaches without words.

Her slow measured gait

Feels the Way.

She gifts courage

TODAY

O God,

May I be your cup

Proffer your gift of Love

Mother your sons and daughters

Sister your lovers

Be child of your embrace

Mirror your likeness

Face, time, place

Echo your Heartsong

Out of Silence.

KOAN

While walking beneath tall trees

One cannot tell wind from rain

Until it strikes you

Which?

Either

There is no difference.

SHADOWS

Dark Matter

Dark, Dark Matter
Secret far from mind
Some far galaxy, rather
Some far, far galaxy, rather
Holds the key to find
What mind cannot grasp
Where one may not dwell
Where none may yet dwell.
Secrets from stars!
They tell
They spell
All creatures kind
Already know
Already know
Ancient rhythm's pulse
Hallows
Allowing life
Love avowing.
Dark Matter
Dark, Dark Matter
Dark Mystery
Alive!

Stand on some solitudinal hill
Hear trembling of stars,
Like ice in glasses at a party.
A grand old party it is!
The difference between venture
        and adventure is joining in.
Lift a toast to a billion galaxies, my friend
To dark Dark Matter!

The Psalmist concludes: "My only companion is darkness."
Good! We could do worse.

The Prophet speaks: "Blind we are led on our journey,
By paths unknown we are guided.
Darkness turns into light before us
Crooked ways made straight."
        By black velvet luminescence
        By Dark Matter
            we are held.

Psalm 88, Isaiah 42:16, For Stephen Hawking

Shadow Game

Hello! My name is Hide and Seek

I may not know what games you play

But I will watch you and your way

Borrow, Imitate or speak

Your language, posture, try to greet

Shy shadow "It" peeks every day

Hello! My name is Hide and Seek

I may not know what game you play?

We must partner, dance, oft repeat

Without, within to have our say

Ebony, white, our shades of gray

Become as one by Paraclete

Hello! My name is Hide and Seek

Shadow knows what games we play.

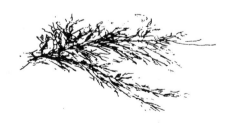

Shadows don't follow

They lead with a push

Glued to soles of Soul

Shadows carry cattle prods

Shove shovels into hands

Ready or not

They come with marching orders
  Dig
  Discover
  Disclose

Shadows admonish:
  Get to work
  Sometimes play

Gotta find a balance somewhere

In the Land of In-Between

Far from Either-Or

In the Place of What-If. . .

That's somewhere east of I-Don't-Care

West of Hooray-I Did It!

South of winter's It-Can't-Be-Done

North of Y'All

AFTER THE STORM
The cry of trees !

Some woke up dead
One afternoon.
Broken sticks, still bleeding
Beg for one more season,
Plead another spring.
Survivors respectfully bow,
Drop their leafy crowns,
Petals on the grave situation,
Look-alikes consoling each other
In the face of a harsh winter.

At the graveyard for trees,
I heard lament
Some not knowing they are dead yet,
Sprout green leaves, pretending roots,
Cannot flower nor seed
Last gasp! Last grasp!
Like painted old ladies in mini-skirts
Flaunting what they don't have.
Transparent illusions.
Yet to discover true beauty –
Yet to discover they can give warmth
At hearths for hearts seeding stories.

Early, early Spring
I search for signs of
     Spring
Are the bluebirds back?
Is the air a little warmer?

Intermittent rain
Imprint of deer in the
     soft soil

First buds on branches
Sound of water in the brook
Yes! The promise of Spring

~ ~ ~

DENIAL

Who would dare to say:

     "The Empress has no clothes?"

If her name was Godiva,

     Would she really care?

Rather ride the horse for all he's worth,

Gallop past those who plead,

     Need and abandon hope

As they see her urgently crossing

Cobbled courtyards.

Watch her erased from their horizons

     Blind – deaf - compulsed.

Who could dare meet her

The other side of the Field of Discontent

Oblivious to her lathered mount?

He stumbles, falls, has spent all.

Can she be found?

Not

Unless she so chooses

Feels alone

The cold wind

at Mirror Lake.

To My Unborn Brother

To my unborn brother
   Whose place I took
      Embedded in uterine wall,

I see now the reason
   You forsook
      The role of being eldest.

Your offspring is a young oak growing
   In rich soil far away from
      Our father's mourning, his rage.

He planted its parent and his intentions
   Most of which he kept
The oak commemorates his gentleness
   His dimpled smile
      He may not have had for a son.

In caring for daughters and our mother
   He almost found himself,
      healed.

We parented those whose children we are,
   We and you who might have been
   But who, by Wisdom's invitation,
      Moved aside.

I weep and call you, Hero. Elder Brother.

Legacy for a Friend

On this Feast of Monica
A mother's tears bequeathed
To daughter
In this sad glad hour undone
Memories come
Become fittingly that which
Doesn't yet seem to fit
A new garment
Fashioned from grief
Woven of all strands, colors, textures.
The Weaver takes the shuttle, saying
"Rest
Abide in my love.
    Now, knowingly.
    All that has been
    All that will be
    Is held for all
    For all Eternity."
    Remember Birthdays into Heavendays
    Are the Grand surprise.
God know it takes some getting used to
Both sides

Feast of Monica—August 27

71

~ ~ ~

Who stands with God
at Judas' tree?

Who cradles God,

Mourns with whispered
love:

"I know, I know, I know",

Rocking in the silence of
choice?

One day I may be bent

Crumpled

Weeping

As with God at Jesus' cross

Or Judas' chosen tree.

When all is said and done

In silence, I must ask

Only to hear again

The answer

In The question:

Could I live other than my call to love

to listen another into their voice -

their choice?

Share God's sorrow

Eclipsing joy?

Be cradled -

Share God's lament -

"I know, I know, I know. . . "

Regret having ever left God alone to mourn.

I think not,

Feel much,

Choose life again.

Judas or my friend - may not have died in vain.

Companion Pieces

That so great a growing thing as tree
Should bow before the likes of me?
"Ah, but true, " I hear her say.
"My feet are rooted in the clay,
My branches sweeping in the air
While you dance about to everywhere."
May we exchange benevolent glance
And both see God, become entranced
By each one's story, each one's song
Exchanging fruit when we come upon
One another in forest glen
Be blessed as we part again.
                              9/9/97

That so great a growing thing as
                    tree
Is felled before the likes of me!
No longer rooted in the clay
Branches stilled that once held
                    sway
Aloft in breezes that caressed
Gently rocked new life in nests.
Yanked, torn, ripped from ground
Powerful wind! Tornadoes sound!
And after - stillness - sad
                    goodbyes
Questions hurled at clearing skies.
An answer's found in forest glen:
Watch! Tree, from seed, begins
                    again.
                              9/15/98

77

Walk
Softly walk

Walk in moccasins
      Out one gate
      Through another
      Into Holy Morning
      Calm, grayed, undefined

Listen to bird-whisper
      Raucous crows and crickets muted
      Hush! Shhhh. . . .

Walk
Walk in moccasins damp
Forward
      Cautious if not bold
      Foot-feel into silky shroud of dew

Silent sentinels pierce the mist
      Great herons (they might be blue)
      Part uncertainties
      Leave wonder in their wake
      Invite trust indivisible

Walk
Softly, surely
Walk in moccasins
      Wearing fog, a moist cloak
      Toward clandestine blessing
      By Sun.

AMIDST THE SEASONS

Juniper Tree

Still in its place

Delivers its progeny

Seeds, filled with grace

By bird seeding south

And for whatever worth

By pen, word of mouth

For those left up north

Who strike match to your

incense

Or brew up a tea

To heal, or reveal

The Mystery.

Moon waned

Lost weight every evening
    Slipped silently away
        Disappeared
Shyly returned
From behind cloud curtains peeked
A silver sliver
    Onto daylight's bright blue stage
    Began to grow,
        wax in confidence
        Once again a full happy face
        At which coyote howled,
            Stirred up mischief among the
            stars
        Lapped up the Milky Way.

Transient birds fly south

First leaf falls, a harbinger

Of the season's change.

Haiku at Mirror Lake

Autumn leaves must turn
At Mirror Lake. God allows
Them to fall, not you.

An autumn pathway
Invites trust of deep
places
Beneath reflection.

Autumn afternoon
Sun's warmth gives way to
chill
Winter moving in

Only one leaf left
Clinging to the topmost branch
Will it fall today?

Silence surrounds me
A gust of wind shakes
leaves free
They fall soundlessly

83

Indian Summer

Make my summer Indian
A rug of red and gold
Purple, white and muted greens
Where tall brown "birds' nests"
Once Anne the Queen's
Bend in symmetry
Across fields exploding
With grasshoppers,
Clicking crickets,
Presided over by monarchs migrating
Attended by yellow retinue.

A tree of life is woven
By variegated birds
Robins and wrens,
Flickers and phoebes
Flock timely – finely
Dining with towhee and thrasher
Warblers, wood sparrow and cedar-wax
Winging their repetitive design – South.

Make my summer Indian
Where flyways cross September's stream
A rivulet to May's
Where eclectic breezes twirl
Twisting leaves from branches.
They tapestry the forest floor.
No moccasin, hoof or paw walks silently.
Walnut and hickory shed heavy trove,
Treasure for creatures, small and large.
A substantive dye!
Slant sunbeams – gold ghilims,
Deftly opened by the Weaver of Seasons. >>>>>>>

>>>>>>>>Make my summer Indian
        The shrinking days
        The longing nights
        Toward winter's quiet thought
        Where wait yarns to be spun
        By warm fires.
        There the shuttle passes,
        The beat is steady on the beam.
        The pattern will inch toward spring
        And summer of another color.

Outside in this dark
night
A Prowler
Stealthily makes rounds
Death stalks, branches,
        blossoms, leaves.
Would the post office post
a sign:
NOT
WANTED:
Jack Frost
But summer
stolen
is mere
exchange
Ransom
awarded:
Magnificent
color
Come
daylight
Come
Daylight

Come!

Walk On a November Day

My sycamore tree
Eclectic, late blooming
Leaves large, small
Up or down
Some still green`
        Though sparse at crown
        They push to grow
        Dare frost and freeze
        Defy the inevitable.
Others yield
        Tumble earthward
        Turn rich patina, brown
        Turn as fine tanned leather
        As fine tanned leather, shining
Shining, worn and rubbed
Like my rich brown buffalo bound
        Bible that tells me of Amos
        Another dresser of sycamores
        Inspired to preach
                elsewhere
        As faithfulness required
        When he would much rather
        would have stayed at home.
                This herdsman and
                dresser of sycamores.

87

A Sonnet

WRITER'S BLOCK—WINTER

This morning, I must write my way
to redemption. New fallen snow
white-papers, erases yesterday.
Here-to-fore unseen tracks outflow
from this stuck place.
Silent sentinels - deer –rabbit,
agents of grace
have turned, trod out of habit,
their footprints, leading strings of love
into Forest-Not-Yet-Revealed.
Forgetfulness of where I was!
Curiosity? Maybe healed,
I take my pen,
Begin again.

Hills Clouds Trees

Clouds
Wind
Blows
Chills
Whispering trees
Not quite bare
The oaks
Without care
Yield to breeze
Until
now
And Wind
Shroud
Still~~~~~~~~
Amidst the
Evergreening
Night, so silent,
    we sing
Our invocation
To the One-Already-
Not-Yet
"O Come
    Emmanuel!"

This Advent

May we be among
"The people on tiptoe with
    expectations"*
And if we be found asleep
At some poor shepherds' fire,
Startle us with angel song
The highest kind.
Draw us along our roads
to the House of Bread
Bethlehem, torn.
Stable fed, perchance,
We will return
And if to sleep or only dream
    Peace on Earth,
Be forever changed by The
Child
And changing a world
    from despair
      to hope.

*Luke 3:15

"Midwinter season
is its own spring."

T. S. Eliot

My heart springs at the sight of snow

Falling

Wrapping a tarnished world

In forgiveness.

White nights oppose dark skies

Chart pathways

Through my house

From my window into trees.

Stars cannot compete

With earth-cloud brilliance.

Moonbeams bounce

Moonface mirrors

Scatters

Doubles the forest, by shadow.

Beneath an ermine mantle

Hope seeded in autumn

Stirs beneath decay.

Secrets suddenly shift,

Whisper of the almost ready

But not yet revealed.

Shhhhh. . . .

Not too soon

But in the fullness of time

Winter will be a memory.

T. S. Eliot; "Little Gidding", line 001:

Psalm to Springtime Sun

O Sun of Spring, wrap us all
In your fiery love's embrace.
Long enough has frosty Earth
Been host to Winter's cold.

Like mourners at Lazarus' wake,
We shout with joy that Earth
Is free of snowy shroud.
Obedient to her God,
According to primal pattern,
She rises once again
From Winter's grave,
Seeking her bright lover
In gleaming Sky.

O beautiful springtime Sun,
Daily Earth soaks your warmth,
Calls to Resurrection
All who sleep in caves
Or linger half-awake in lifeless clay,
All who wait your quickening call.

May your caressing warmth,
Bring greening Resurrection
Be a sacrament and sign,
That I too shall be touched by Fire,
Awakening from my earthen
        hibernation
To live in endless light
In the Eternal Spring.

Upon Occasion ~ ~ ~

   The color and texture woven into our lives often come from times we are especially aware of the spirit-connect. It happens. It happens when just around some TURNED CORNERS we meet others who bless, challenge, coax us forward. We take that next step ahead, held in part by the confidence of a companion who may evoke latent gift or call us to accountability.

   These persons mediate the Presence and God's best hope for us. May we name them in our prayers of gratitude and live what they teach us for the poetry of our lives.

~ ~ ~

A Letter to Madeleine

You called – coaxed – challenged,
Loved this writer into life.
With each "Yes!" - "Good!" - Why not . . .
    "Find it" or
"You moved with ease and grace into . . .",
  By your faithfulness to your muse,
      you example me to heed my own.
With each "I had fun reading . . ."
    "I'm glad you had fun writing!"
    "This lovely piece . . ."
    "Send it!"
          or
    "What if . . .?"
I sent my first book.
    "So like you."
And then another.
Madeleine, you are
          Clan mother – midwife,
          Mapmaker – faith keeper,
          Teller of the God-story,
          Keeper of the God-dream,
Living both angel and faith as verbs.

What a privilege to be caught in the updraft
          with you for some of the
          "veriest" weeks of my life!

As always, with gratitude and sawdust in my shoes.

                    M.B. to Madeleine L'Engle, 1988

Once Upon a Mailbox

One day I will know
More about Galaxy NGC 1316
Or Lagoon Nebula
But for Now it is a scheme
To fascinate, by U. S. Postal Service
Incredula!

I, too, write more than I know
Commemoratively
Stamp, send
With abandon, into rain, wind, fire, snow
Toward whatever end
Or is it a beginning?
I trust not so much to the finite
As to the Infinite
Infinite will transport
To a receptor's heart
What we both know
Beyond knowing
Beyond words
Beyond galaxies
Beyond time
For both of us.

Postmarked by a starry night's
Promise to deliver
My word river of intent.

Postscript on an envelope to a friend.

Evaluation

On this delicious afternoon
Poetry is precious.
Once deemed luxury,
it's well nigh necessity. Before,
I did not allow indulgence
which meant, I'll not take wine
save on occasion.
Now, on doctor's orders
when I dine there is a glass,
sometimes two.
Some recent Doctor of the Church
French, Therese of Lisieux,
perhaps, can prescribe.
Write a slip which
saves my poor deprived heart
when taken: POETRY DAILY
It may awaken
what lies sleeping,
barely beating,
bring strength enough to
rosy-cheek the WORD
waiting, pulsing, hoping for "Yes!"
Yes! So I've heard.
and Jessica smiles.

For Jessica Powers, poet, met at one turned corner.

Eulogy For Tom

A bright young star

Has left out constellation!

Jettisoned by cosmic calamity.

Our shaken planet teeters

Toward Chaos

Rails

Reels
Against a Black Hole.

Stand apart from being

Sucked into its vortex!

Pulsars – young luminaries shine,

Bright shoots of Everlastingness,

Chips off the not-so-old

Asteroid, we will miss.

They settle into new orbits

By navigation of angels.

~ ~ ~

New Boots

While walking from the Upper Meadow down

Toward the Chapel glen

My new boots began to untie themselves.

Anticipation?

Then in the cedared hallow place

Our soul/soles were both exposed.

Barefoot in the Holy

Bare of feet, wholly

My new boots!

My new boots and I

      Are breaking in.

My new boots, <u>Made in China</u>

Tie me to others' stories

The hidden language of women

From Hunan Province

Curiously, it is called

<u>Nu Shu</u>

I hear an echo:

      My sisters' laughter.

Assent to Nascent Ascent

Gold
Silver ribbons
Hieroglyphics
Ancient language
Erased by satin curtain

Theater
Appears less to no more
Past stage and stages

Uplifted to soar
To Source
Playing peek-a-boo
Around cloud pillows
Among Angel feathers
Becoming Light, as One

Glimpse as turned
From diminishment
Mountains as hillocks, thinly seeded
Giant trees as saplings
Outcropping rocks as pebbles
Thrust above snow carpet
Soon to be waterfall

Tears

Beneath this storied flight
Others' tasks to stroll
In awe among
Bright prisms
Pieces of Everlastingness

Red, yellow, orange blossoms
Strewn across a desert floor
Silently seed
Wait through essential seasons
Nascent.

Nascent – 1. Beginning to exist or develop.
2. The condition of an element at the
instant it is set free from a combination
in which it has previously existed.

Kaleidoscope

We know not the mind of God; rather we experience the heart of God that knows us. The heart of God's mercy - compassion - is love. The love we experience through one another is a God given glimpse of the all pervasive all embracing, all empowering love God has for us. The love that we are gifted to share with one another speaks of the one great vitality that really matters.

We may not always have loved wisely, but let it be understood we cannot but ultimately have loved well. God, our creator, sustainer, transformer, receives all the pieces of our lives, fashioning them into a uniquely patterned kaleidoscope. We have only to look to glimpse the beauty by holding it to the Light.

Angels: Ang + EL (Hebrew) = Messengers of God. They direct our attention to the holy in ordinary things around us. These images can become icons that bring us home to our truest selves in touch with the Divine.

Image Angels

Have strong striped wings.

Today one visited
        Unseen of course
Left a tangible talisman
        In my path.

I was walking
        Somewhere
I forgot
        Somewhere

        Walking

          Walking

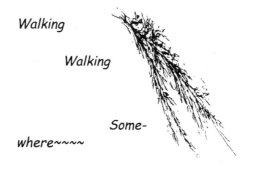

            Some-
where~~~~

        ~~~~~Lost~~~~~~~~~~~~~

Found
~~~~~~~~~~~~~ Feather flown~~~~~~~~~~~~~~~~~
                 Home.

What happens when I listen

To the deepest place

Within me?

How do I begin to go there?

Someone

Gave me a clue

One to walk with

Who
Knows my real name

From which I may turn

Away

Pretending not to hear.

To turn

Around is dizzying.

I will fall.

There is no going back

So I stand

On the tightrope of paradox.

Give me a balance bar

Please

And keep beckoning.

Talk me across the chasm.

Someone!

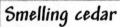

Smelling cedar

Transports
Closed eyes
Into the Tabernacle
Where silence whispers
Presence enfolds
Where heart-speak
      Is spoken
Sung for inner ears.

A Eucharist

Morning walk on a blacktop road
Table spread after an all night rain
Altar for earthworms
This sacrifice is for the birds!
Invocation!
Invitation!
"Take and eat -
This is my body given up for you."
Pardon my irreverence?
No!
"All that came to be was alive with God's life.
No single thing was created without..."
There appeared the sun.
There appeared the hawk -
Hawking the wares.
A feast! A banquet!
Gift from the night
There appeared the sun.
Illumination!
Transubstantiation!
To taste and see
How gracious the Word is enfleshed
On a morning walk
A morning dance
On a blacktop altar
After an all night rain.

Matthew 26:26; John 1:3

111

112

At a Place of solitude

OXYMORON

Beware of the oxymoron

Which dwells in this place,

Begetting essential luxury,

Serving in secret grandeur,

The bountiful fasts that

Dryly assuage the salivating thirst

Of souls who seek without looking,

Ask without words,

Knock silently

At shuttered windows,

All the while picturing in clear obscurity

The complete becoming

With the blink of their inner eye

In the night,

Thereby awakening to day.

A silent exclamation:

"Oh!"

Beware of being aware.

ENCOUNTERS ~ ~ ~

Two deer or was it one twice
I saw on the woodland trail?
In the morning, it enticed
me to pause and to avail
the timeless longing
of my shackled soul,
to sense belonging.
Its gaze ennobled,
bestowed a gentle blessing,
an invisible mantle
for my shoulders, cushioning
the yoke of the day until
deep in the ferns, as night de-
scended,
our reunion was God intended.

~ ~ ~

Today,

I saw the feet of Christ
In open-toed sandals
     and closed,
In polished black wingtips
     long and narrow,
In short brown oxfords, scruffy
     tennies - just the same;
On new clacking heels, staccato,
And dragging, limping,
     cane accompanied.
In patent leather tiny dancing slippers
     skipping,
With long purposeful strides
     confident,
In shuffling old gait
     hesitation steps,
With adolescent bravado
     shod in red, blue, black, brown,
     green, white
     and dingy-color-long-gone.
Today, I prayed in the first pew off the
     aisle
     Having come from the altar -
My soles exposed, holes and all
     to those who knelt behind me.

Magdalen *Even as she wept, she stooped to peer*
inside and there she saw a dazzling sight,
         more than she expected.
After all, throughout her night of sorrow,
She could not leave neglected
The poor vestiges, the body shell
         so cruelly treated.
She knew not where, were it not for one
         she did not know,
A Joseph who had pleaded
Her friend from his cross.
Life gone, as once was known

                    Into a black dawn, angels shone,
                         questioned.
                    She turned, confronted by a
                    gardener who further probed:
                    "Why are you weeping?"
                         She railed: "Isn't it
                         enough that he is dead!
                         Gone! Gone! Gone!
                         Now where has what was
                         left been taken?"
                    Then she heard her name, a
                    familiar cadence and inflection.
                    And she ran — was first—to tell
                         other mourners
                         how she saw
                    The Gardener of her soul,
                         her Rabboni!
His return was certain, secure,
         as she stooped to peer
Inside herself.
A tomb no longer,
         but a room
         filled with dazzling light.

On our own terms we sail

Trusting the weighted keel

Of unspoken life

To guard against capsize

Until the test.

A raging storm snaps the mast

Drowns our sail

Our hopes and expectations

Of making our port of choice.

Never-the-less we weigh anchor

In a calm harbor

Navigated by Mystery.

As in a dream
                toward morning

                On a quiet beach

        Small waves, rivulets ~~~
                Whisper-lick toes
                Shift sand
                Gift shells, starfish
                and polished blue glass

        Eyes gather other treasures

        Several silent Masai
                Slim, statuesque
                Step from their long log-boat
                Carry tall poles

        Turn away from shore's certainty
        Stride confidently
        Water walk
        Almost glide
        Heads erect
        Display confidence
                The depths will support them
                        Toward their destination.

FOR MY COMPANION

Barefoot
Hear the muffled yearning of the human heart
Listen it to clarity
For deafened ears
Become unstopped
By a single question
Inflection?
Word forms – stutters into voice
Before the single solitary flame
Poised
Before enkindled portent
Shh~~~~
Posture silence
Attend
Incarnation begins/continues
With each and every yes –
Yes
Yes?
YES!
To God's whispered invitation
Hear the muffled yearning of the human heart
Partnered with Divine
Hear it into voice
Stand longing on its feet
Send it forth
Give thanks
Smile
O yes!
Remember your shoes
Before walking on.

After Words

As was tradition, in their homes in winter, my ancestors gathered to tell their stories, reciting their triumphs, mourning their tragedies. Laughing or crying, they wove a bond of relationship with the land, each other, and their understanding of their Creator. Other northern plains dwellers shared this common custom.

Outside near their doorways stood solitary stalwart cedar juniper trees, growing where they were planted as house blessings. Long after the people who planted them and many of the stories were laid to rest, long after the dwellings had fallen into disrepair or were appropriated for other uses, the cedars have stood, bent, sculpted by seasons of change.

I remember being told as a child that my great grandfather, a carpenter, always planted a juniper near the entry to each new home he built. Was this practice something he learned from Native Americans who enacted a similar pattern at their lodges? Or is it something universal? In the midst our own generation, we seek sign, plant symbol, tell story, compose song and become poets because we must.

126

No Telling

What we'll be spelling

After Last Telling

At Epiphany

We may live

In anticipation

Of manifestation

Fashioning our destinies

Spelled to WORD

Enchanted

Spelled to WORD

Forward

From this time forth

Forevermore

So be it

So be it

Be so

From Spaces for falling
              through   ~~~
    What is it to BE? ~~~

From a list of random words— perhaps one from each
journal page (or the daily newspaper will do), discover
the healing power of metaphor.

~ ~ ~

Who Am I?

Some call me Gentle Wind,
        Not knowing how I chafe
                at the ropes that bind me.
But, in my Spirit House at Full Moon rise!
        In my Spirit House at Full Moon rise,
        Moon, a melon to be carved appears!
        One stroke of the pen-knife releases
                a fountain of words ~~~
                Jasmine scented.

Masks dissolve on my Island of Solitude.
        There is a bottomless well.
        There is a bottomless well.
Ashes from bridges burned behind
        are strewn across the water ~~~ the snow.
The ghetto which once imprisoned
        is on some other side
                of Dreams become real.
Cousins Hurricane Wind and Jaguar no longer imperil.
        They are free,
                but do not make free with me.
I have found the Dolphin inside.
        I have found the Dolphin inside.
        She is wise, compassionate,
                playful ~~~ ~~ ~
        We pluck a peach from the water-tree,
        Share the fruit
                Plant the stone
                Discover the lost glove.

The lost glove.

        It warms my writing hand.

129

With Gratitude . . .

Beyond sense of personal privilege at being inspired to write these poems, I offer this book with gratitude, thanksgiving and applause.

Gratitude for encouragement, tolerance and wise counsel of mentors, family and friends, especially from Post Scripts Writers' Guild, without whom this book would not have come to be.

Thanksgiving for the disciplined editors:
Ann Grossmayer, Barbara Skypala,
Joan Hallaron, Teresa DiLenge and
Valerie Downes of Sakura Press

Applause for readers who have played and prayed with this journal, making it their own.

Martha Bartholomew
Siloam
18N600 West Hill Rd.
Dundee, IL 60118

junipertree170@msn.com

130

This Poet

   Martha Bartholomew, is a retreat guide and spiritual companion from her home Siloam Retreat - House of Prayer near Dundee Illinois. There, *TURNED CORNERS* are wooded trails inviting exploration. Undergraduate studies in art, religious studies and spirituality yielded both B.A. and M.A. degrees for her from Mundelein College and Loyola University in Chicago. She holds a Doctor of Ministry from The Graduate Theological Foundation, Donaldson, IN. and has been involved in pastoral ministries for many years. She has published in numerous periodicals and owns to being a weaver of fibers as well as *words*. She is an Associate member of the Sinsinawa Dominican Congregation. Martha is married, a grandmother, and a member of Postscripts Writing Guild.

OTHER BOOKS YOU MAY ENJOY INCLUDE:

John Fox
Poetic Medicine: The healing Art of
Poem-Making.
Jeremy P.Tarcher / Putnam Inc. New York.
© 1997

Jane Hirshfield
Nine Gates: Entering the Mind of Poetry.
Harper Collins Publishers Inc. New York
© 1997

Susan Goldsmith Wooldridge
Poemcrazy:
Freeing Your Life With Words.
Random House Inc. New York
© 1996